Fuck Puppies

By Felicia Biznatch

Disclaimer: The following is my personal perspective. If it doesn't align with yours, that's perfectly fine; we can agree to disagree. Now, buckle up for a ride through the comically chaotic world of puppies and babies...

So, you thought you stumbled upon an adult-themed escapade, huh? Well, I hate to break it to you, but this isn't the place for that. The X-rated adventures are in a different part of town, dimly lit, with suspicious-looking patrons furtively exiting with black bags in tow. This book isn't about that; it's not bestiality snuff literature.

Why, you ask? Because, my friends, this is about the challenges of dealing with tiny Houdinis who have zero control over their bodily functions — yes, the infamous puppies.

Now shall we begin?...

Fuck puppies!

oh, and just for fun,

Fuck Babies too!

(ha ha ha ha! see we're having fun already)

The Great Escape Artists

Fuck Puppies!

In case you're wondering why I say, "Fuck puppies"? It's not a declaration of hatred; it's a survival mantra.

These little furballs are the Houdini's of the animal kingdom, minus the top hat and cape. They've mastered the art of escaping and have zero control over their bodily functions.

Picture this: a tiny canine magician passing gas so loud it could rival a trombone, followed by a startled leap, a spin, and a frenzied tail chase. It's like living in a circus where the main act is a slapstick comedy performed by adorable, fuzzy jesters.

"Furry Mayhem and Tiny Terrors"

Why the exasperation with puppies, you ask? Well, aside from their impressive Houdini skills, they have also decided that my humble abode is their personal toilet – a realm of doggy delights and disasters.

These little furballs, in their quest for mischief, have turned my living room into their own special edition of "Puppy Potty Paradise." It is like they attended a masterclass in home decor, but instead of choosing tasteful rugs and elegant furniture, they opted for a Jackson Pollock-inspired approach.

Every corner of the house is fair game – a canvas for their artistic expression in the medium of pee and poop. It is as if my once pristine floors have become a gallery displaying their avant-garde bodily fluid installations. And trust me, they are prolific artists: there's no limit to their creative output.

So, picture this: you are tiptoeing through what used to be your cozy living space, now transformed into a minefield of surprises. It is like navigating a labyrinth, except instead of a Minotaur, you're avoiding puddles and surprises left by the mischievous furry architects of chaos.

But fear not! For we are just scratching the surface of the wild antics of these little troublemakers.

🐾

Ugh!

Fucking puppies.

Babies and Puppies – Wrecking Ball Wonders

"Oh, you thought you could have nice things?

"You are so funny!"

No, I am Afraid you can no longer have nice things. and the ones you have now well pretty soon you won't have those either. It's sad but the hard truth.

Better I tell you now, because the fact of the matter is, puppies are like tiny demolition people with a penchant for chaos. Buying a new couch is like inviting them to a buffet — they cannot resist sinking their teeth into the delicacy of upholstery. It's a challenge to keep the living room looking less like a home and more like a furry construction site.

Attempting to keep the house tidy with these little fur hurricanes is like trying to juggle water balloons – messy and almost guaranteed to end in disaster. Imagine buying that one pair of shoes you've wanted forever. You know the ones you paid a ton for, and you absolutely love, you wore them once maybe twice.

You've got plans for the night and you have picked the perfect outfit, and you know exactly what shoes will tie it all together. You go to get them for your closet and (que the horror music) one if not both have a had a complete makeover from hell like they were a volunteer model for a Mary kay party. Destroyed and unrecognizable.

Spoiler alert!

The puppies were mad because you left them, and those shoes are the last things they remember you leaving the house in. Cannot leave if you don't have shoes.

Oh, by the way, good luck finding another pair just like them. Because the shoe company is no longer producing these particular pairs of shoes but there is a similar pair that are not even close to the ones your precious puppies have made into their own personal chew toy and not near as comfortable.

No, I am afraid that is just one of the many irreplaceable items you will lose.

I suggest you start staking out a place bury all the precious Items you love now. Because they will all become a large graveyard soon my friend and FEMA does not help with this kind of disaster I'm afraid.

And then there are the babies – tiny ninjas of destruction. They have mastered the art of making a clean room look like a tornado passed through. It is a collaboration of chaos and a duet of disorder.

So, if you are daydreaming about a Pinterest-worthy home, get ready for a reality check.

These adorable troublemakers will turn your house into a playground of pandemonium. But hey, who needs a perfect home when you can have a daily comedy show starring the fur-covered jesters and their miniature partners in crime? Welcome to the circus of calamity, where chaos is the star of the show.

If You have yet to experience either of these little bundles of terror then consider this your warning guide. but if you are in my boat and have 1 or both or multiple of either of them. you can totally relate to what I am saying here. its okay you can admit it!

I mean come on why else would you be here. It is okay. I won't tell. It will be our secret. I am not judging. I get it.

Ha ha ha ha we all get it.

I digress, now where was I?

Oh yes I remember....

Cry, Whine, Repeat – The Symphony of Parenthood

"Fuck puppies!" Why? Because they are the Mozart of mischief, composing a masterful symphony of whines and cries that echo through the halls. It is like living in a canine opera, where every bark is a note, and every howl is a dramatic crescendo.

If you hear a cry, it is not just a noise; it's a performance, and you're in the front row.

And then there are the babies – the tiny maestros of mayhem. Their cries could rival a rock concert and calming them down is like trying to negotiate peace in the middle of a tantrum tornado. It is a daily drama, a soap opera of squalling that keeps you on the edge of your sanity.

Now, imagine this: you are basking in the serenity of silence, and suddenly, the banshee cry begins. It is not just a disturbance; it's a full-blown vocal hurricane that leaves you questioning the choices that led to this cacophony. But fear not, for this is the soundtrack of parenthood, a melodic reminder that your peaceful days are on permanent hiatus.

So, if you ever feel the urge to make eye contact with a crying puppy or baby....
Well.

Actually, just don't do it.

Really!

Hey, I am serious! do not look at them.

Don't do it!.............

You did it didn't you...
Well, I tried to warn you.

I Guess this is where I leave you. Have fun. hope you get to finish this someday. It's really good. You can always try the audio version.

For those of you who actually took my advice.

Let us all take a moment to remember Karen who fell for the banshee's call.

And laugh. ha ha ha ha not getting us! Suckers! Bah ha ha ha haha. Later Karen.

Moving on...

Fuck puppies...

And Babies.

Little Dictators;

Welcome to Parenthood

Puppies and babies, the adorable dictators of our lives. Once they enter your home, consider your freedom officially on house arrest.

You used to be the CEO of your life, but now you're demoted to the position of Mom or Dad, with no board to answer to, except a diaper-changing committee.

Remember Karen?

The ambitious spirit who once had dreams and aspirations. Well, say hello to Little Baby Gage and Cujo's mom. It's not just a title: it's a 24/7 job with no coffee breaks and plenty of messes to clean up.

These tiny despots come with their own set of rules and regulations. Forget your plans: their agenda is the only one that matters.

You're no longer an individual.

You're now the personal assistant to a pint-sized CEO who communicates mainly through cries and barks.

It's a regime change that no one saw coming. Your once spontaneous life is now a carefully scheduled operation.

Your to-do list involves everything from changing diapers to negotiating with tiny terrorists about bedtime.

But fear not!

For in the world of these little dictators, every negotiation is a game of rock-paper-scissors where they always win!

So, welcome to parenthood. Where you're not the boss anymore. Your new title is a mix of chauffeur, chef, and chief negotiator.

May the odds be ever in your favor.

Baby Talk:
The Chuckle Factory of Cuteness

Now, instead of sticking to grown-up talk and regular English, we've collectively decided to take a whimsical plunge into the realm of "widdle wishy-washy baby talk."

Picture it:

A high-pitched dialect featuring an accent I've playfully dubbed the "Gigglefication" accent – a language so delightfully complex that even language aficionados find themselves scratching their heads.

Now hold on to your hats because it's not just with puppies.

Even those sweet widdle baby wabys are caught up in the linguistic whirlwind.

"Who's an adorable widdle baby? *You are, you are!*"

This becomes the anthem as we embark on a mission to nab

those irresistibly tiny toes.

It's as if every day is a laugh-out-loud adventure into our newly adopted "widdle wishy-washy baby talk," where grown-ups transform into linguistic magicians. Sentences dance in the silliest way possible and you, my friend, become the headlining comedian in this uproarious stand-up club of delightful gibberish.

But hold your laughter...

There's more.

The adorable gigglefication accent isn't just a vocal switch. It's a full-blown transformation that turns everyday conversations into a side-splitting spectacle.

So, gear up for a linguistic rollercoaster where every word is a punchline, and the punchline is, well, pure cuteness.

Fuck Puppies and their adorable little faces.

I mean seriously how can you stay mad at a face like that? They could be tiny little terrorists sent to take over your world, and we would let them. Because of their precious little faces, people would say." This is bad, really bad.

Awe but They are just so darn cute. How bad can it really be?"

And those Fucking babies, just so dang cute they do and say the darndest things.

Picture this, your telling that adorable little tyrant "No no, sweety do not touch that". Then they stop, look you in the eye with a straight face and do it anyway.

Then before you can get mad, they just laugh that super precious little laugh they all have and say,

"uhoh."

Then just crawl off like, "clean this mess up and don't ever tell me how to live my life again".

"It's my nap time and I'm hungry, now if you don't mind, I think I'll retire to my crib now." and off they go crying for no reason. On the verge of a total meltdown.

With the unspoken warning of.

 so,f I were you, I would hurry up and feed me so I can fall asleep, and you can

get some cleaning done¨

Toute de suite, Lady!

FUCK! Puppies!

The sleepless nights, never ending headaches, trashed house.

AND THE YARD!

Let's just say goodbye to that lush green grass, and those beautiful flower beds. I know how hard you worked on them.

Car seats, couch cushions, side panels on the car doors, the dry wall in your house. Destroyed!

"I can see right into little Susy's room now." "Who needs baby monitors."

"I always wanted to put a doggy door in the laundry room." "I just didn't realize it till now."

Said no one, ever!

Fucking babies.

🐾🐾

They might get a pass on the yard and flowers but as far as the rest....

Nope!
Ugh,

I fucking hate puppies....

And babies!

Fucking puppies,
And their hair.

In everything!
On everything!

All I know is if you are not a fan of shedding, you are now.

From now on this is your life.

You will eat, sleep, breathe, and WEAR their hair.

It's going to be everywhere, and your friends and family are going to just love it.

(Just kidding, everyone is going to hate it.)

Or.... just get a poodle.

Or, a poodle mix. I hear they don't shed.

Unfortunately, there's no hope for your baby because it will grow and get bigger and then they too will shed.

Especially if it's a girl. But that's another book.

Don't get me started on teenagers they might be worse than babies and puppies combined.

Well save that for another time.

So, Disgusting!

Okay so babies get a pass on the shedding

on this one. A temporary one. Congratulations Babies 1 point for you.

Anyways....
Those fucking puppies,

And those gross fucking BABIESSSSS!!!!! Someone please explains to me why they always have sticky little hands and fingers.

There can be absolutly no jam, syrup, any sticky substance whatsoever even anywhere in the vicinity of them; yet they have jam hands and what do they do with them?

They want to put them in your mouth or on your face. Just touch you period. It's like a horror movie.

I can see it now those tiny little monsters begin to ooze this sticky unknown substance from their fingers and mouth, and they are coming for you.

"OH NO RUN!"

Because all they need is to touch you and instantly the sticky ooze starts to spread all over you.

It goes in your mouth, in your hair, your pockets, your purse or whatever bag type personal item you have on you that holds your money and everything else you or anyone could ever need.

Pliers, super glue, granola bars. Personal identification, etc.

I digress.

"Ahhhhh! Everyone run for your life!"

" Ewe, Gross!", Don't touch me!"

"Does anyone have some wet ones, anyone"?

"Hand sanitizer, even?"

"Anyone, come one help me out, its just smearing and spreading everywhere!"

Soon you've been completely consumed by the sticky ooze and if they aren't stopped the ooze will consume the world!

For the love of God please wash your babies jam hands! Or night of the living ooze won't be just a bad dream but your waking nightmare.

Do you know what the absolute worst Part Is About Fucking Puppies and Babies is?

We can't really say fuck puppies or babies.

I mean What would people think if we said that aloud! Besides deep down no matter how much you want to hate them, or think you do.

You don't really. They are adorable, sweet, loving precious little gifts. And once you get one you don't know how you ever lived without them. I mean what would life be like without them?

I'll tell you what it'll be like!

There would be less hair in everything as well as on everything.

lawns would be lushes' green grass instead of mud and holes to break and ankle in. that girl's

/guy's trip to Vegas you wanted to go on, well now you can.

That concert three hours away on a weeknight you had to pass on. No one asking you for something 24/7.

People will call you by name, no more being beckoned a million times a day sometimes they'll do it out of habit and don't even need anything or they forgot.

MOM! MOM, M OM! HEY MOM, HELLO MOM, MOTHER, MOMMY. You can go to the bathroom alone, watch whatever you want, never again will you have to hear but why can't I have that when everyone else has one, why can't I go, why, why, why.

less headaches, more sleeping, no more drool puddles to step in, eaten shoes, your stuff won't get trashed or broken, no more crying, and wining, blah blah blah blah blah

blah blah blah blah blah blah blah blah blah blah ....

❖ Note to the readers from the author:

I hope you enjoyed this book, for the record I don't really hate puppies or babies. I have two dogs and a child of my own that I live for and can't live without same goes for my dogs they are my furry children. Sometimes I like my dogs more than my kid and vice versa. Being a parent is a big deal and also an honor and privilege. Same goes for being a pet owner. You are responsible for these little lives and when you are a parent your job is to raise them right, protect them from harm. Love them and guide them down the right path so they can grow up and do the same. They don't come with manuals and lots of things you won't get to redo so if you fuck up or miss it. Well, I guess there's always the next one. Right? I'm just kidding. My point is love them with all your heart and remember they didn't ask to be here with you. You did, however, when you brought them home. So, treat them right, and if you had it rough. Remember how you felt and break the cycle. Because as cliché as it may sound, it still rings true. They are our future. Let's make it a better one.

Thanks for reading.

I DEDICATE THIS BOOK TO:

MY PUPPIES,

MYMOM,

MY SON 💕

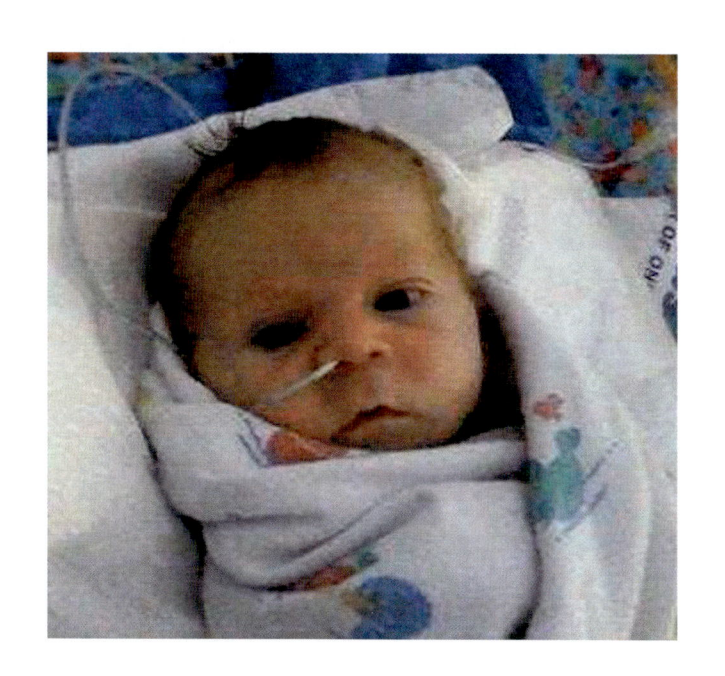

And last but never least my best friends.

To whom without them this wouldn't have been possible. (Thanks Babes, both of ya!)

Made in the USA
Columbia, SC
14 February 2024

5bbc3ded-c097-4447-aed1-16f0aa1921e8R01